Milet Publishing
Smallfields Cottage, Cox Green
Rudgwick, Horsham, West Sussex
RH12 3DE England
info@milet.com
www.milet.com
www.milet.co.uk

First English–German edition published by Milet Publishing in 2013

Copyright © Milet Publishing, 2013

ISBN 978 1 84059 793 6

Original Turkish text written by Erdem Seçmen
Translated to English by Alvin Parmar and adapted by Milet

Illustrated by Chris Dittopoulos
Designed by Christangelos Seferiadis

Printed and bound in Turkey by Ertem Matbaası

My Bilingual Book

Sight
Das Sehen

English–German

How do we see colors on a butterfly's wings?

Die schillernden Farben auf des Schmetterlings Schwingen -

Let's think about how we see things . . .

Denken wir einmal nach, wie sehen wir die Dinge? . . .

Our eyes show us everything, like faces,

Unsere Augen zeigen uns alles: Gesichter,

colors, actions, places . . .

Farben, Taten, Lichter. . .

Giraffe has a coat of brown spots on yellow.

Die Giraffe trägt ein gelbes Fell mit braunen Flecken,

Watch him bend to say hello!

um Hallo zu sagen, muss sie den Kopf herunter recken.

Our eyes can show our feelings.

Unsere Augen können Gefühlen Ausdruck verleihen,

We see Panda's eyes are smiling.

Der Panda zeigt mit den Augen sein Lächeln und kein Weinen.

To see, we need more than our eyes.

Um zu sehen, brauchen wir mehr als nur Augen.

We need light at night to help us spy.

Bei Nacht muss ein Licht uns helfen zu schauen.

Owl can see in a different way.

Eine Eule sieht die Welt auf ganz andere Weise,

Even in the dark, he can spot his prey.

selbst im Dunkel wird Beute für sie zur Speise.

Seeing through glasses? Now I'm perplexed!

Die Schrift verschwimmt? Da gibt's keine Pille!

When our eyes need help, we give them specs!

Brauchen die Augen Hilfe, tragen wir eine Brille!

Tears are not only for sad or happy,

Tränen zeigen nicht nur, wenn wir froh oder traurig sind,

they help keep our eyes moist and healthy.

sie halten die Augen feucht und gesund, das weiß jedes Kind.

Our eyelids spread our tears when we blink,

Unsere Lider verteilen die Tränen beim Blinzeln,

and we use them to sleep and to wink!

schließen sich, wenn wir schlafen oder ganz kurz, wenn wir zwinkern.

We close our eyes when we're asleep in bed,

Wir schließen die Augen, wenn wir nachts im Bett träumen,

but in our dreams, we may see orange, green, red . . .

und sehen doch orange Möhren, rote Äpfel und grüne Bäume . . .